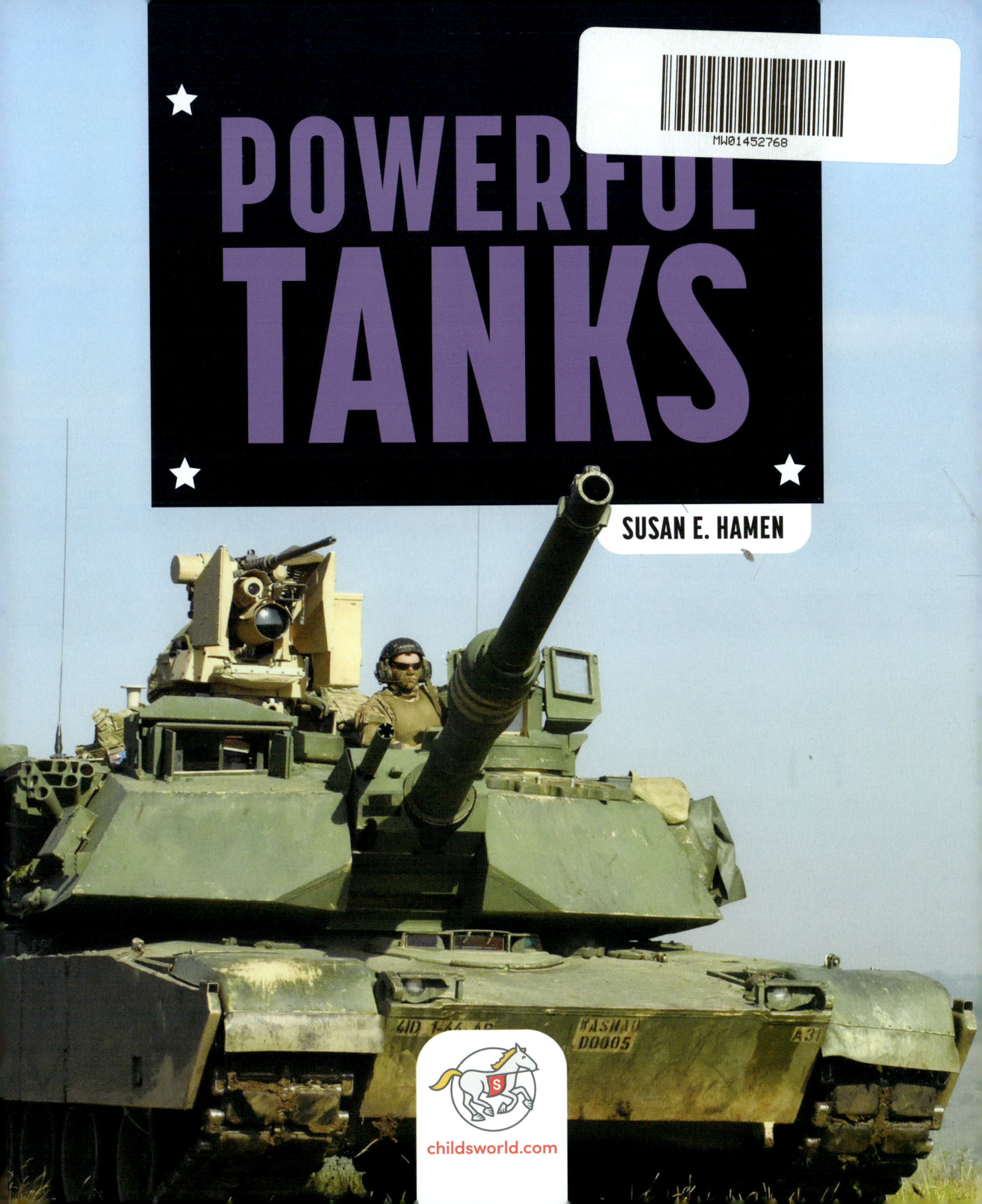

Published by The Child's World®
800-599-READ • www.childsworld.com

Copyright © 2024 by The Child's World®
All rights reserved. No part of this book may be reproduced or utilized in any form or by any means without written permission from the publisher.

Photography Credits
Photographs ©: Spc. Kelsey M VanFleet/US Army Europe and Africa/DVIDS, cover, 1; Spc. Randis Monroe/Fort Irwin Operations Group/DVIDS, 3; Thomas Alvarez/Idaho Army National Guard/DVIDS, 5; Sgt. Sarah Kirby/US Army, 6; Sgt. Ken Scar/7th Mobile Public Affairs Detachment/US Army, 9; Shutterstock Images, 10; Sgt. Emmanuel Ramos/15th Marine Expeditionary Unit/DVIDS, 13; Gunnery Sgt. Rome Lazarus/11th Marine Expeditionary Unit/DVIDS, 15; Army Cpl. Alisha Grezlik/US Army, 16; Cpl. Gabrielle Quire/Marine Forces Reserve/DVIDS, 17; Lance Cpl. Jason Morrison/1st Marine Division/DVIDS, 19; Staff Sgt. Austin Berner/982nd Signal Company/DVIDS, 20

ISBN Information
9781503816671 (Reinforced Library Binding)
9781503881433 (Portable Document Format)
9781503882744 (Online Multi-user eBook)
9781503884052 (Electronic Publication)

LCCN 2022951210

Printed in the United States of America

ABOUT THE AUTHOR

Susan E. Hamen lives in Minnesota with her husband, Ryan, and her son and daughter. Hamen is the author of more than 30 books for children. Some of her favorite topics have included World War II, ancient Rome, and what the world was like before online shopping and social media. She'd like to thank John C. Wall Jr., 1SG US Army (RET) for sharing his experiences and expertise with the Abrams tanks to help with the writing of this book.

CONTENTS

CHAPTER ONE
MEET THE M1A2 ABRAMS TANK 4

CHAPTER TWO
ON THE OUTSIDE 8

CHAPTER THREE
INSIDE THE HATCH 14

CHAPTER FOUR
POWERFUL WEAPONRY 18

Glossary . . . 22
Fast Facts . . . 23
One Stride Further . . . 23
Find Out More . . . 24
Index . . . 24

CHAPTER ONE

MEET THE M1A2 ABRAMS TANK

As the sun rises, the US Army tank crew prepares for training at Fort Stewart, Georgia. They enter their M1A2 Abrams tank and roll out to a training field. The tank climbs a small hill and stops. Its **turret** rotates. One shot fires from the tank's gun. The explosive boom rings across the field. The **round** leaves the gun at about 3,500 miles per hour (5,600 kmh). The blast sends the round 2 miles (3.2 km) away. The target explodes.

The tank moves through the nearby woods and sets up for another shot. Inside the tank, the loader feeds more **ammunition** into the gun. The gunner aims the gun at a far-off target. Another shot blasts across the field. The force of the shot jolts the tank backward a little. When the round hits its target, the wood and concrete blocks explode. The driver quickly moves the tank to aim at another target.

Training missions that use real ammunition are called live-fire exercises.

Each soldier in the tank's crew practices driving the tank, loading its weapons, and firing its guns.

Members of the crew continue their training in the powerful tank. They work hard on their drills in case they have to take the tank into battle. They practice in all kinds of weather conditions. Drivers gain experience driving the tank on roads, grass, hills, mud, snow, and even ice-covered paths.

The M1A2 Abrams is the main battle tank of the US Army. It holds a crew of four people. The crew includes the commander, driver, ammunition loader, and gunner.

The tank is 32 feet (9.8 m) long and 11.5 feet (3.5 m) wide. It stands 8 feet (2.4 m) tall. It was designed to be shorter than earlier tanks so it could avoid being hit by incoming rounds. The Abrams weighs more than 62 tons (56 metric tons). That is more than 35 average-size cars. It holds 500 gallons (1,900 L) of fuel. Although it is very heavy, it can move at speeds up to 42 miles per hour (68 kmh). Because of its speed and quiet engine, the tank has been nicknamed "Whispering Death."

The M1A2 Abrams tank entered service in 1992. It was named after General Creighton W. Abrams Jr. He was a commander in the Vietnam War (1954–1975). The US Army owns and operates about 900 M1A2 Abrams tanks. These replaced an older version called the M1A1. One M1A2 costs approximately $8.92 million to produce. The tank is expected to remain in service until at least 2050. It is one of the most powerful tanks in the world.

THE POWER OF NAMES

Tank crews are allowed to name their tank. Some interesting names have included "Cruel Intentions" and "All You Can Eat." One tank that was captained by a woman was given the name "Barbie's Dreamhouse." What name would you choose for your tank if you were part of a crew and why?

CHAPTER TWO

ON THE OUTSIDE

The main body of the M1A2 Abrams is called the hull. It has armored side plates on both sides that are designed to protect the tank's wheels. Caterpillar tracks wrap around the seven wheels on each side of the tank. Each caterpillar track is made of many treads linked together. These treads are made of steel and have replaceable rubber pads attached to them. There is a **sprocket** on each side of the tank, too. Each sprocket keeps the caterpillar tracks turning on the wheels. Gear teeth on the sprocket help move the treads. The caterpillar tracks allow the tank to drive over bumpy, steep, and uneven **terrain.** It can cross large holes or trenches in the ground, too.

The side panels on the Abrams can fold back. This allows people to access the tracks for maintenance.

PARTS OF AN M1A2 ABRAMS TANK

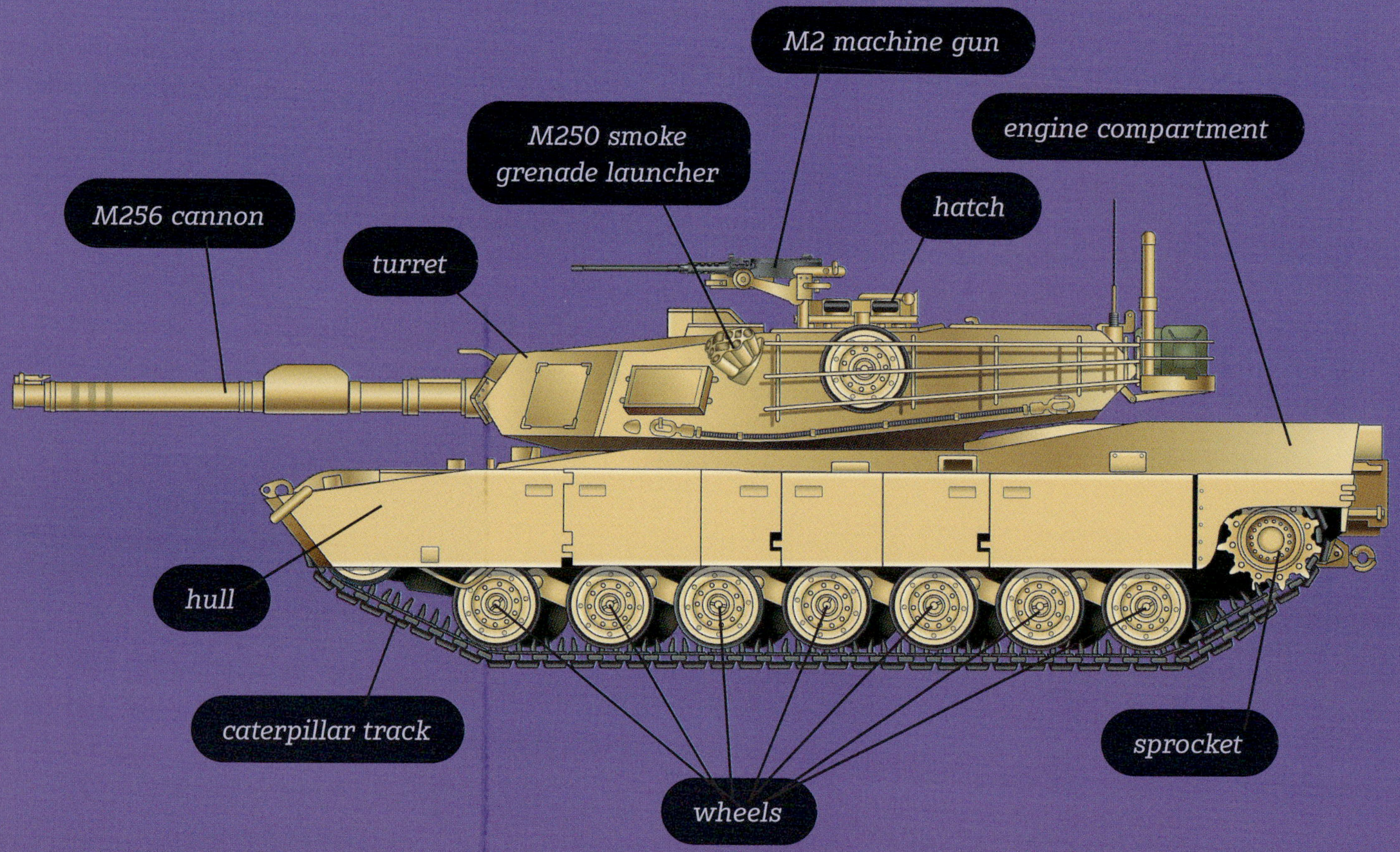

- M256 cannon
- turret
- M250 smoke grenade launcher
- M2 machine gun
- hatch
- engine compartment
- hull
- caterpillar track
- wheels
- sprocket

The Abrams has lots of important parts. Any piece of the tank can be replaced if it breaks.

The Abrams is built with a material called Chobham armor. This gives the tank its strength. The exact ingredients of this material are top secret. But people believe it is made up of layers of nylon micromesh, titanium, and ceramic bonded together. At the front and top of the hull, a mesh made of depleted uranium is added. Depleted uranium is a very dense metal. It offers protection against anti-tank weaponry. In addition, the sides of the tank are angled to help **deflect** incoming enemy fire from the tank. All of these things help the Abrams withstand heavy firepower.

DRIVING WITH CATERPILLAR TRACKS

The M1A2 Abrams tank moves across rough terrain very easily on caterpillar tracks. The driver doesn't steer the tank like a car. Instead, he changes the speed of the tracks. To turn left, the right treads need to move faster than the left. The left treads need to move faster to turn right. The driver controls the speed of the treads with two hand controls.

The engine is at the back of the tank. When repairs are needed, the entire engine compartment can be lifted out of the tank. The engine works similarly to a jet engine. It can run on different types of fuel, but jet fuel is most often used. The Abrams tank uses about 1.7 gallons (6.4 L) of gas to drive 1 mile (1.6 km).

On top of the tank is the turret. The turret can rotate all the way around in about nine seconds. It also holds the tank's weapons. A phone on the back of the tank lets soldiers outside talk to the tank crew inside.

Before phones were added to the Abrams, soldiers had to open the hatch and shout over the noise of the tank's engine to communicate.

CHAPTER THREE

INSIDE THE HATCH

The inside of the M1A2 Abrams is very small. It is tight quarters for the crew. The commander's hatch and the loader's hatch both lead straight down into the turret basket from the top of the tank. The turret basket is where three of the four tank crew members work. The gunner sits on the right side and works the gun and weapon controls. The commander sits directly behind the gunner. The loader stands to the left of the main gun.

The commander tells the driver where to steer the tank and which direction to go. He can see in every direction outside of the tank through the viewing ports. A **thermal** imaging system allows the commander to see at night. The system creates an image based on the different amounts of heat given off by objects in the field of view.

The commander can see the tank's surroundings on a display inside the tank.

Commanders can open their hatches to communicate with other tanks during training missions.

The gunner controls the tank's cannon. Behind the gunner are doors that lead to storage space for the rounds. The loader reaches back to pull out a round and then loads it into the cannon. The interior and top of the turret are specially designed. If a round accidentally explodes, the explosion goes up and out of the tank instead of toward the tank crew.

The driver is in the tank's lower body, under the turret basket. Because of the cramped space, the driver lies back in the seat. The driver uses a T-bar hand control and two brake pedals to steer the tank. The driver's seat is accessed through a hatch in the hull. There is also a very small escape hatch that leads into the turret.

The driver has a display panel that shows the tank's speed and location, as well as information about the engine.

CHAPTER FOUR

POWERFUL WEAPONRY

The M1A2 Abrams tank has remarkable defenses and is built to withstand a lot of damage. But it is also armed with powerful weapons of its own. The main gun on the turret is a 120 mm M256 cannon. The cannon can hit targets up to 2 miles (3.2 km) away. The rounds that are loaded into it are almost 5 inches (13 cm) wide, up to 39 inches (99 cm) long, and weigh 40 to 50 pounds (18–23 kg).

The Abrams is equipped with special automatic **stabilizers** that allow the guns to stay locked on a target. Even when the tank is moving across rough terrain, the main gun remains steady. The gunner can load different kinds of rounds into the main gun. Some rounds are designed to destroy buildings and structures. Others can disable or destroy enemy tanks. The gunner even has rounds that can be shot up into the air to illuminate the area at night.

Most M1A2 Abrams tanks carry 40 rounds for the main gun.

18

The M2 machine gun can be fired by the gunner or the commander.

On top of the turret, an M240 machine gun is mounted next to the main gun. This gun fires in the same direction as the main gun. The gunner can fire this machine gun while inside the tank. Another M2 machine gun is mounted on the turret. This gun can be fired by the gunner either inside or outside the tank.

    The Abrams is fitted with M250 smoke grenade launchers on each side. These smoke grenades make it hard for the enemy to see the tank during combat. The smoke masks the heat that the tank gives off. This makes it harder for the enemy to attack the tank using heat-seeking weapons. Launching smoke gives the crew a chance to move out of danger. It also gives the crew an opportunity to more safely escape a damaged tank.

    The M1A2 Abrams tank is an incredible military vehicle. It can easily drive across rocky, uneven, or steep terrain. There are several impressive weapons on the Abrams, and it has strong defenses against enemy attacks. Advanced technology even makes the Abrams capable of driving safely at night. It has proven to be one of the most powerful tanks in the world and continues to outperform enemy tanks on the battlefield.

ammunition (am-yoo-NIH-shun) Ammunition is a supply of bullets and rounds. In the M1A2 Abrams tank, there is one person who is in charge of loading ammunition.

deflect (dih-FLEKT) To deflect something means to make the object go in a different direction than it was originally going. The Abrams tank's armor is angled to deflect enemy weapons.

round (ROWND) Round is another word for a bullet or missile shot from a weapon. When the round hit the target, it exploded.

sprocket (SPRAW-kit) A sprocket is a toothed wheel that helps turn chains or tracks. A sprocket on each side of the Abrams tank helps turn the caterpillar tracks.

stabilizers (STAY-buh-lye-zers) Stabilizers are devices that keep things still. Tank stabilizers keep the guns steady across rocky surfaces.

terrain (tuh-RAYN) Terrain means an area of land and its natural features. The tank can drive across rocky terrain.

thermal (THUR-muhl) Thermal means that something is related to heat. The thermal image shows that the soldier is warmer than the grass around him.

turret (TUR-et) The turret is a small revolving structure on top of a tank with guns mounted on it. Most tanks have a turret that can rotate all the way around.

FAST FACTS

★ The M1A2 Abrams is the main tank used by the US Army.

★ The interior of the tank holds a crew of four people: the tank commander, driver, ammunition loader, and gunner.

★ The M1A2 Abrams is 32 feet (9.8 m) long and 11.5 feet (3.5 m) wide. It was designed to be shorter than previous models so it would be harder for enemies to hit.

★ The tank holds 500 gallons (1,900 L) of fuel. The Abrams uses about 1.7 gallons (6.4 L) of gas to drive 1 mile (1.6 km).

★ The M1A2 Abrams tank can travel up to 42 miles per hour (68 kmh).

★ The M1A2 Abrams tank was nicknamed "Whispering Death."

ONE STRIDE FURTHER

★ What do you think would be the biggest challenges of being part of a tank crew?

★ What personality traits do you think make for a good tank crew member and why?

★ As weapons continue to advance, what are some design changes you think will happen for future tanks?

★ Can you think of any weaknesses that tanks have? When would it make more sense to use a different vehicle or type of equipment?

FIND OUT MORE

IN THE LIBRARY

Leed, Percy. *The US Army in Action.* Minneapolis, MN: Lerner Publications, 2023.

Ringstad, Arnold. *Powerful Missiles and Bombs.* Parker, CO: The Child's World, 2024.

Tank: The Definitive Visual History of Armored Vehicles. New York, NY: DK, 2017.

ON THE WEB

Visit our website for links about tanks:

childsworld.com/links

Note to Parents, Caregivers, Teachers, and Librarians: We routinely verify our Web links to make sure they are safe and active sites. So encourage your readers to check them out!

INDEX

ammunition loader, 4, 6, 14, 16

cannon, 10, 14, 16, 18, 20
commander, 6, 7, 14

driver, 4, 6, 11, 14, 17

gunner, 4, 6, 14, 16, 18, 20

M2 machine gun, 10, 20
M240 machine gun, 20

rounds, 4, 7, 16, 18

tracks, 8, 10, 11
turret, 4, 10, 12, 14, 16–17, 18, 20